Street by Street

C000115425

CAMBRIDGE

COTTENHAM, GREAT SHELFORD, HISTON, SAWSTON, WATERBEACH

Bar Hill, Barton, Bottisham, Cherry Hinton, Comberton, Duxford, Fulbourn, Girton, Grantchester, Harston, Haslingfield, Milton, Trumpington

3rd edition July 2007
© Automobile Association Developments Limited 2007

Original edition printed May 2001

  This product includes map data licensed from Ordnance Survey® with the permission of the Controller of Her Majesty's Stationery Office. © Crown copyright 2007. All rights reserved. Licence number 100021153.

The copyright in all PAF is owned by Royal Mail Group plc.

Published by AA Publishing (a trading name of Automobile Association Developments Limited, whose registered office is Fanum House, Basing View, Basingstoke, Hampshire RG21 4EA. Registered number 1878835).

Produced by the Mapping Services Department of The Automobile Association. (A03128)

A CIP Catalogue record for this book is available from the British Library.

Printed by Oriental Press in Dubai

Ref: ML108y

Junction 9	Motorway & junction		17	Page continuation 1:15,000			Cinema
Services	Motorway service area		2	Page continuation to enlarged scale 1:10,000			Golf course
	Primary road single/dual			River/canal, lake, pier		▲	Camping AA inspected
Services	Primary road service area			Aqueduct, lock, weir			Caravan site AA inspected
	A road single/dual carriageway		465 ▲ Winter Hill	Peak (with height in metres)			Camping & caravan site AA inspected
	B road single/dual carriageway			Beach			Theme park
	Other road single/dual carriageway			Woodland			Abbey, cathedral or priory
	Minor/private road, access may be restricted			Park		✗	Castle
← ←	One-way street			Cemetery			Historic house or building
	Pedestrian area			Built-up area		Wakehurst Place NT	National Trust property
	Track or footpath			Industrial/business building		Ⓜ	Museum or art gallery
	Road under construction			Leisure building			Roman antiquity
	Road tunnel			Retail building			Ancient site, battlefield or monument
P	Parking			Other building			Industrial interest
P+	Park & Ride		Madeira Hotel	Hotel AA inspected			Garden
	Bus/coach station		A&E	Hospital with 24-hour A&E department			Garden Centre Garden Centre Association Member
	Railway & main railway station		PO	Post Office			Garden Centre Wyevale Garden Centre
	Railway & minor railway station			Public library			Arboretum
	Light railway & station		i	Tourist Information Centre			Farm or animal centre
+++++	Preserved private railway		i	Seasonal Tourist Information Centre			Zoological or wildlife collection
LC	Level crossing			Petrol station, 24 hour Major suppliers only			Bird collection
	Tramway		†	Church/chapel			Nature reserve
	Ferry route			Public toilets		V	Visitor or heritage centre
	Airport runway			Toilet with disabled facilities			Country park
	County, administrative boundary		PH	Public house AA recommended			Cave
	Mounds			Restaurant AA inspected			Windmill
	City wall			Theatre or performing arts centre			Distillery, brewery or vineyard

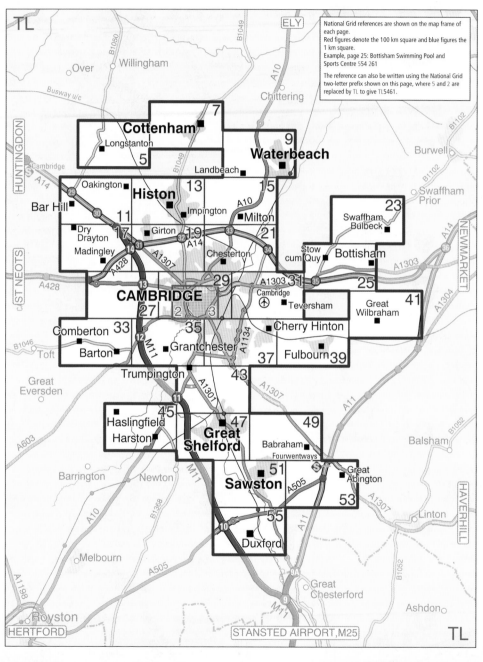

National Grid references are shown on the map frame of each page.
Red figures denote the 100 km square and blue figures the 1 km square.
Example, page 25: Bottisham Swimming Pool and Sports Centre 554 261

The reference can also be written using the National Grid two-letter prefix shown on this page, where 5 and 2 are replaced by TL to give TL5461.

TL

Over   Willingham

ELY

Busway u/c

Chittering

HUNTINGDON

Cambridge

Cottenham

7

Longstanton

Waterbeach

9

5

Landbeach

Burwell

Oakington

13

15

Swaffham Prior

Histon

Impington

23

Bar Hill

Milton

Swaffham Bulbeck

11

Dry Drayton

Girton

17

19

21

36

Madingley

Chesterton

Stow cum Quy

Bottisham

NEWMARKET

ST NEOTS

CAMBRIDGE

29

31

25

Cambridge ✈

Teversham

Great Wilbraham

41

27

2   3

Comberton

33

35

Cherry Hinton

Barton

Grantchester

Toft

37

39

Fulbourn

Great Eversden

Trumpington

43

Haslingfield

45

Great Shelford

47

49

Babraham

Balsham

Harston

Fourwentways

Barrington

Newton

Sawston

51

Great Abington

HAVERHILL

53

Melbourn

55

Linton

Duxford

Great Chesterford

Ashdon

Royston

HERTFORD

STANSTED AIRPORT, M25

TL

Enlarged scale pages   1:10,000

6.3 inches to 1 mile

0   miles   1/4

0   kilometres   1/4   1/2

Scale of main map pages   1:15,000

4.2 inches to 1 mile

0   miles   1/2

0   kilometres   1/2   1

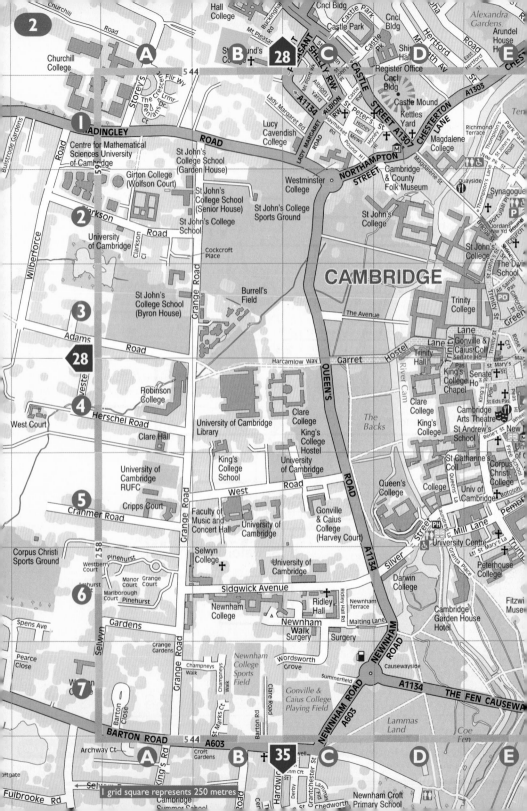

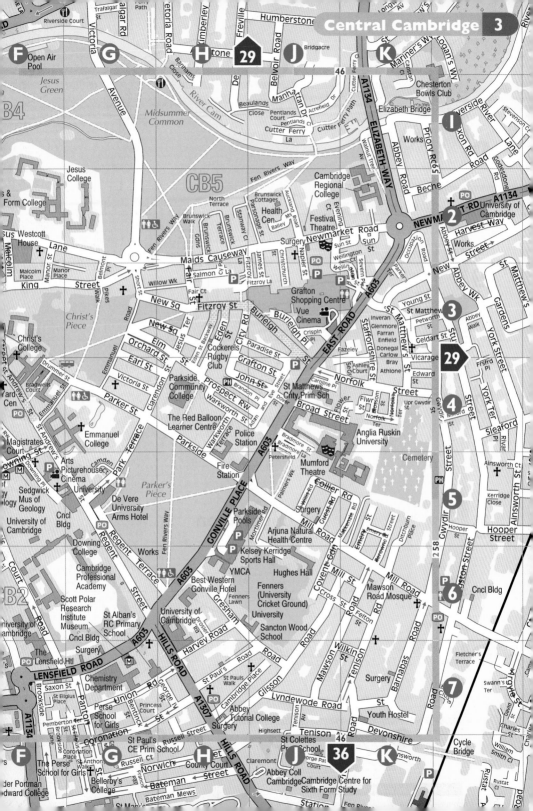

4

New Fa[r]

A   B   C c   D

539   40

Over Road

68

1

Over Road

STATION

Pathfinder Long Distance Walk

67

2

Cambridge Golf Club

Golf Course

Ladywalk

Sheepwash Way

HIGH ST

B1050

Brookside

Hatton Park Community Primary School

Stevensons Rd

3

Magdalene Close

Rampton

Colesfield

Hatton's

Thornhill Pl

Magdalene Cl

Cemetery

HATTON'S ROAD

High Street

Hatton's Cl

Thornhill Pl

Rectory Cl

266

Longstanton

The Dale

PO

✝

4

B1050

School   Lane

Woodside

Thatchers Wd

Mills

Clive Hall Dr

St. Mi

Thatchers Wood

5

Wilson's Road

St. Michaels

Longstanton Road

✝

A   B   C   D

539   40

1 grid square represents 500 metres

E   F   G   H

41   42

High Street

King Street

Orch End

Home F.681 Close

Rampt

I

6

Brook Field

Reynolds' Drove

Cuckoo Lane

2

The Hol

okfield Farm

Rampton Road

CB4

Rampton Drift

Rampton Drift

Rampton Drift

Guided Busway u/c

67

3

Westwick Field

4

2 66

Lambs' Cross

5

E   F   G   H

41   42

Oakington Road

Road

Westwick

6

A B C D

Cow Lane

5 43 44

69

Great North Fen Drove

Great North Fen

New Farm

I

2

Cow Lane

High Street

Orch End

Ho 6.88 Farm Close

Church End

Street

Rampton Road

3

Rampton

5

Little North Fen

North Fen Farm

4

Drive

267

The Holme

The Rowells

5

Oakington Road

5 43 44

A B C D

Westwick Field

Further or Farm Field

I grid square represents 500 metres

Albrough Farm

TWENTY

Cottenham Lode

Church Close

Church Lane

Natt Street

Broad Lane

Sames Court

Courtyard

Males Close

Broad La

HIGH STREET

B1049

Kingfisher Wy

Tenison

The Spinney

Kestrel

Broad

Lane

Eversden

Bullfinch Cl

The Close

Dunnocks

The Wrens

The Linnets

Goldfinch Dr

Sug St

The Herons

Surgery

Cambridge Regional College

COTTENHAM

Rooks Street

Margett Street

CS Cl

Goode Cl

Corbett St

Crowlands

Victory Way

Lane

Franklin Gardens

Telegraph St

Cundell Dr

New Road

Rooks

Coolidge Gardens

Coolidge Cl

Calvin Close

PO

Harlestones Rd

Lyles Road

Denmark Road

Lacks Close

Beach Road

Cemetery

Pelham Cl

HIGH ST

Brenda Gautrey Wy

Leopold Wk

Sovereign Wy

Brenley Wy

Pelham Way

Lee Cl

Leopold St

Gautrey

Ellis

MFC

Mordans

Bramley

Cottenham Village College

Foundry Close

Cssngtn Cl

Dunstal Fld

Dunstal Field

Short Drove

Beach Road

B1049

Between se Drove

Cottenham Pastures

Cottenham

A **B** **C** **D**

5 47 48

Beach Ditch

1

67

7

Goose
Hall

Ely
Flint
Road
La

2

Overbrook
Farm

A10

Cottenham Road

3

66

Green End

4

Beche Way   Ravensdale

Reubens Road

Rectory
Farm   Chapmans
Close   Spaldings
Lane

5   **Landbeach**

265

Cockfen   Lane   Waterbeach

5 47 48

A **14** **B** **C** worth
ne

Street

E F G H

40 41

Longstanton Road

Manor Farm Close

Church View

Mill Rd

Vicarage Close

I

Meadow Farm

Days Meadow

Da's Meadow

High Street

Water Lane

Queens Way

Cemetery

Lowbury Crs

Coles Lane

The Drift

Croft La

Cherry Orch

Holme Close

Arcadia Gdns

Oakington CE (Aided) School

PO

Mead View

Oakington

Kettles Close

2

Phypers Farm

The Brdwy

Orchard Way

Cambridge

64

Dry Drayton Road

Rd

3

12 Midfield

Poplar Farm

4

263

130

5

Cambridge City Crematorium

40 41

E F G H

HUNTINGDON ROAD 14

17

Catch Hall

Grange Farm

E F G H

44 45 65

I

Mill Lane Farm

Bedlam Farm

2

COTTENHAM ROAD

Mill Lane

Cottenham Road
Alstead Road
Greenleas
Burwett Way
Clay Way
Winders Lane
Nun's Orchard
Normanton Wy
Parlour Cl
Frm Cl
Muncey
Old Farm Walk
Luckett's
Narrow Lane
GLEBE WAY
Orchard Road
Garden Wk
Youngman Av
Narrow Close
Drake Way

64

Manor Farm

3

14

Church St
Bell Hill
Symonds Close
Windmill Lane
Prior's Cl
B1049
Orchard Road
Spring Close
Cem
Paddock Close
Histon & Impington Junior School
Lawson Cl
Ambrose Way
Milton Road
St Andrews Way
St George's
Way
St Grgs Ct

Harding Way
Hill Close
School Hill
High Street
PO
Brook Cl
Dwyers
Joyce
HISTON
Impington
Hereward Close
Bishop Way
Hereward Cl
Lane
Clay Close Lane
Burgoynes Farm Close
Burgoyne's Road
Doctor's Close
Woodcock Close
Percheron Close

263

4

Merton Road
Home Road
West Road
Saffron Road
New School Road
WATER LANE
Station Road
B1049
The Dole
Roselea
Homefield Cl
Holt
Netherhall Cl
The Dole Rd
Hollymoor
New Park Drive
Impington Sports Centre
Impington Village College

Histon & Impington Infant Sch
Poplar Rd
Oak
Hitch
Tree Rd
Love's Close
Kay
Way
Henry Morris
Karlane
Schl La
Ch Rd
Mowlam
BRIDGE ROAD
New Rd
Impington
Histon FC

Chivers Way
WY Cl
Phr
Chivers Road
Villa Road
Villa Pl

5

The Business Cen
Surg
PO
LC

South Road
Villa Road
Crescent Road
Cambridge Road
New Rd
Burrou
gh Fld
The C
Bys

44 45

E F **19** G H

The Crescent
College Road
Mill Road
High R

Guided Busway u/c

Landbeach

E Waterbeach F Road G 9 H WATERBEACH

48 49 65

Mtt Pl Cl
Ams
Banworth
Lane

High Street

Lime Farm

Landbeach Road

†

Stanton Farm

Cemetery

Car Dyke Road

Glebe Road
Coronation Cl B
Cambric
Road

ELY ROAD

I

2

64

Fen Rivers Way

River Cam

3

Clayhithe

4

Fen Rivers Way

263

Clayhithe Road

A10

Ely Road Way

Sutton Cl
Humphries Way
Td Cl
David Bull Wy
Cherry C.
Starling
Willow Crs
G Cl

High St
Knights'
Wy

PH

PO
Church La

† Milton

Dock Lane
St John's La

5
Church End
† Street
Horningsea

Goding Way

Hall End
Old school La
Fen Road
Bt Ct

Street
Road
Wilton Way
Coles
Pryor Close
Shirley Cl
Walking Way

†

E F 21 G H

reation Pearson Close 48 49 High

Abbot
Wy
Priory Road

ship

LC

Fen Rivers Way

ndustrial

Baits Bite

A　B　10　C　D

Pettitt's Cl
538
39

Searles Meadow
Bakers Fld
Pettitt's Lane

Dry Drayton

1

62

Cotton's Fld

Dry Drayton
CE Primary
School

Park St
Park St

ry Farm

2

3

61

4

5

260

Mading
Hall

538
39

A　B　C　D

Park Farm

E
Cambridge City
Crematorium

F

11

G

H

I

HUNTINGDON ROAD A14

40

41

62

Catch
Hall

Grange Farm

Washpit
Road

2

Beck Brook
Farm

The Avenue

M11

Junction 14

3

18

A428

4

University of
Cambridge

PH

Madingley

Madingley
School

New
Farm

5

260

A428

Cambridge Rd

40

41

E

F

26

G

H

Cambridge Rd

Moor Barns
Farm

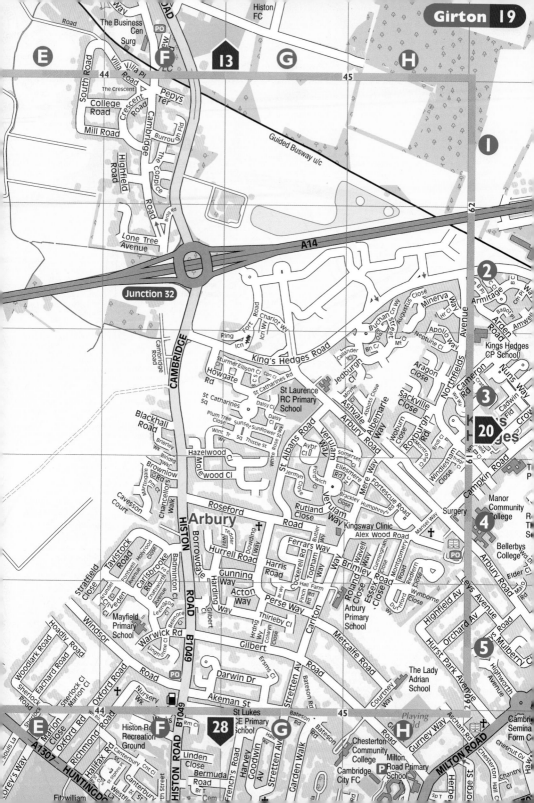

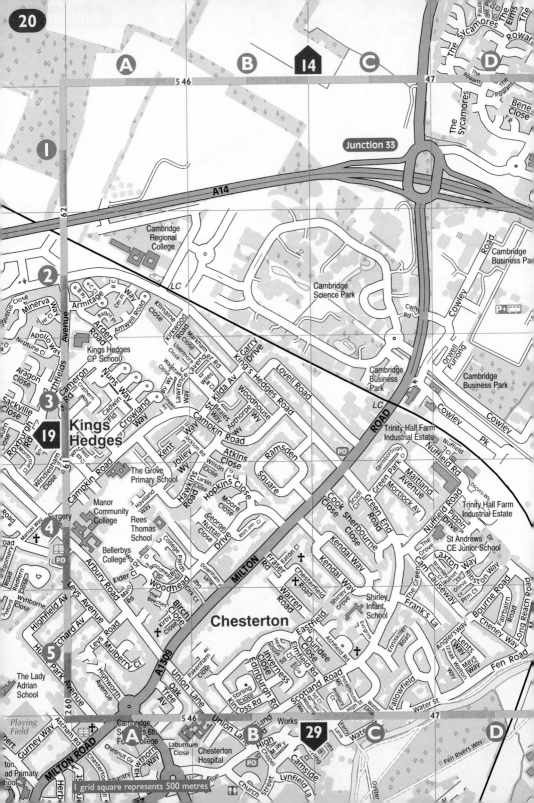

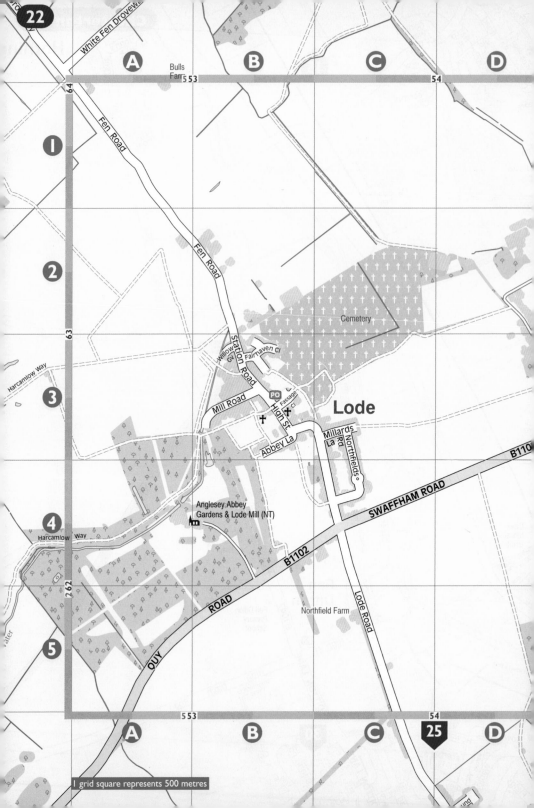

22

A   53   B   C   54   D

White Fen Droveway

Bulls Farm

1

Fen Road

64

2

63

Fen Road

Harcamlow Way

3

Willow Gv

Station Road

Fairhaven Cl

Cemetery

PO

Passage

Mill Road

High St

Cl

Lode

Millards La

Northfields Rd

Abbey La

B110

4

262

Harcamlow Way

Anglesey Abbey
Gardens & Lode Mill (NT)

SWAFFHAM ROAD

QUY ROAD

B1102

Lode Road

Northfield Farm

5

A   53   B   C   54   **25**   D

1 grid square represents 500 metres

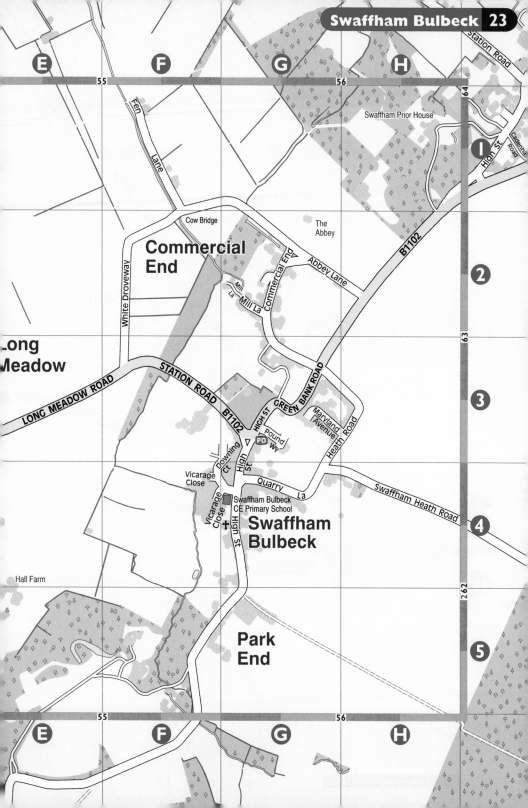

E F G H

55 56

Station Road

Swaffham Prior House

High St

Cadgenth Road

I

Fen Lane

64

Cow Bridge

The Abbey

Commercial End

White Droveway

Commercial End

Abbey Lane

B1102

2

Mill La

Mill La

Long Meadow

LONG MEADOW ROAD

STATION ROAD B1102

GREEN BANK ROAD

HIGH ST

Maryland Avenue

Heath Road

63

3

Pound Wy

PO

Downing Ct

High St

Vicarage Close

Quarry La

Swaffham Heath Road

Vicarage Close

Swaffham Bulbeck CE Primary School

Hall Farm

Swaffham Bulbeck

High St

262

4

Park End

5

E F G H

55 56

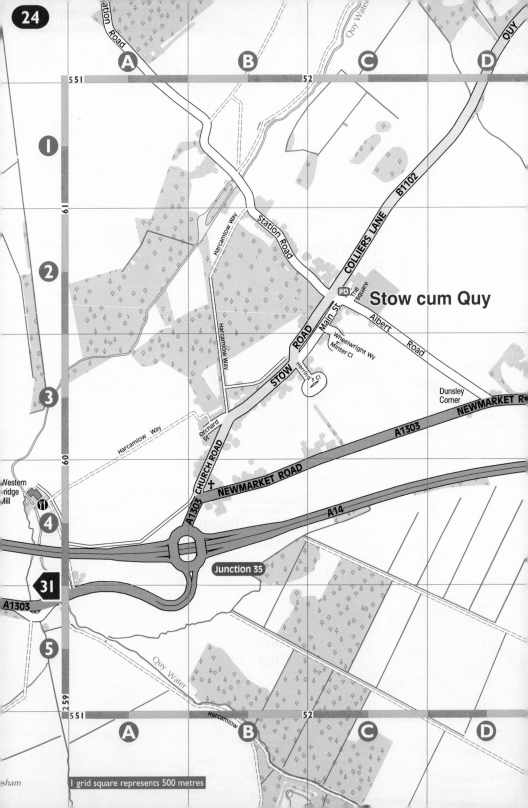

A B C D

551 52 QUY

1

19

Quy Water

Station Road

Harcamlow Way

Station Road

B1102

COLLIERS LANE

2

PO The Square

Stow cum Quy

Main St

Albert Road

Wheelwright Wy

Minter Cl

STOW

ROAD

Herring's Cl

Harcamlow Way

3

Dunsley Corner

NEWMARKET R

Harcamlow Way

Orchard St

A1303

CHURCH ROAD

A1303

NEWMARKET ROAD

✝ NEWMARKET ROAD

60

Western ridge Mill

4

A14

A1303

31

Junction 35

A1303

5

259

Quy Water

551 52

A B C D

Harcamlow Way

sham

I grid square represents 500 metres

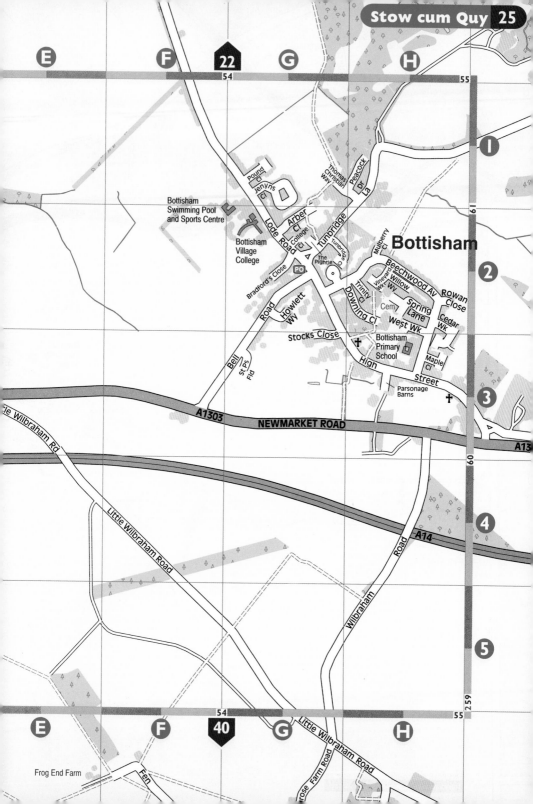

E F **22** G H

54 55

1

Pound Cl
Jenyns Cl

Thomas Christian Way
Christian Way
Peacock La

Bottisham
Swimming Pool
and Sports Centre

Arber Cl
College

Bottisham

Lode Road

Bottisham
Village College

Tunbridge

The Pightle
Tumbridge Cl

Mulberry Cl

Beechwood Av

Rowan Close

2

Bradford's Close

PO

Vineyard Wy
Willow Wy
Trinity Cl

Cedar Wk

Howlett Wy

Road

Dowling Cl

Cem

Spring Lane

West Wk

Stocks Close

Bottisham
Primary School

Maple Cl

Bell

St P's Fld

High

Street

Parsonage Barns

3

A1303

NEWMARKET ROAD

A13

60

tle Wilbraham Rd

Little Wilbraham Road

A14

4

Wilbraham

Road

5

59

54 55

E F **40** G H

Little Wilbraham Road

Frog End Farm

Fen

rose Farm Road

26

A   B   **17**   C   D

5 39   60   40

New Farm

Church Lane

A47

idge Rd

Cambridge Road

Cemetery

1

2   59

A1303   **ST NEOTS ROAD**   A1303

Coton CE Community School

3

Whitwell Way

Church End

Sadlers Close

Benny's Wy

St. John's Rd

St. Peter's Rd

Silverdale Cl

Silverdale Av

Brookfield Rd

C

Whitwell Way

Whitwell Farm

Biu Brook

4

Jaggard's Farm

2 58

Long Road

5

5 39   40

A   B   **33**   C   D

1 grid square represents 500 metres

E F 18 42 G H

Moor Barns Farm

Huntingdon

I

University of Cambridge

MADINGLEY ROAD

Junction 13

P+

Lansdowne Road

Conduit Head Road

MADINGLEY ROAD

University of Cambridge

High Cross

University of Cambridge

University of Cambridge

Madingley

2

Cambridge Road

PO

J. J. Thomson Avenue

Charles

Babbage Rd

Clerk Maxwell Road

Perr

The Footpath

Brook Lane

Harcamlow Way

Harcamlow Way

3

28 Cambridg University Track

4

Grantchester Road

Wheatcases

Gough Way

Pe P

Laundry Farm

5

BARTON

Newn

E F 34 42 G H Queen's College Sports Ground

King's College Sports Ground

Grantchester

A603

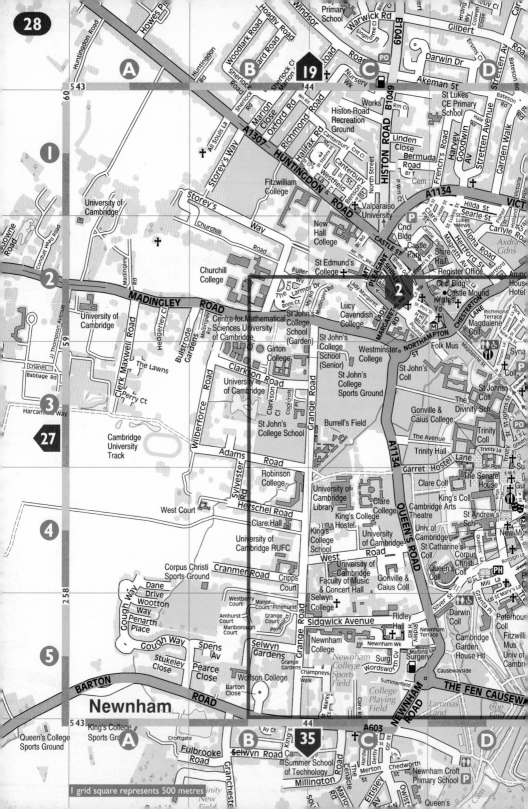

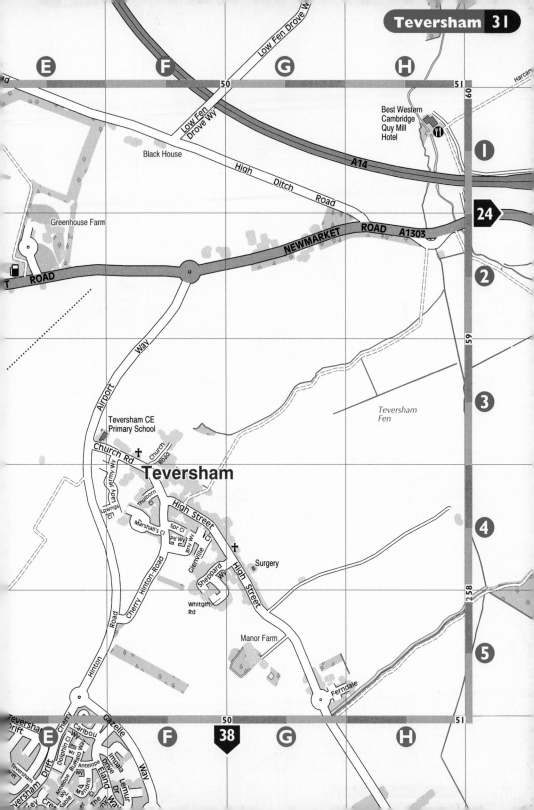

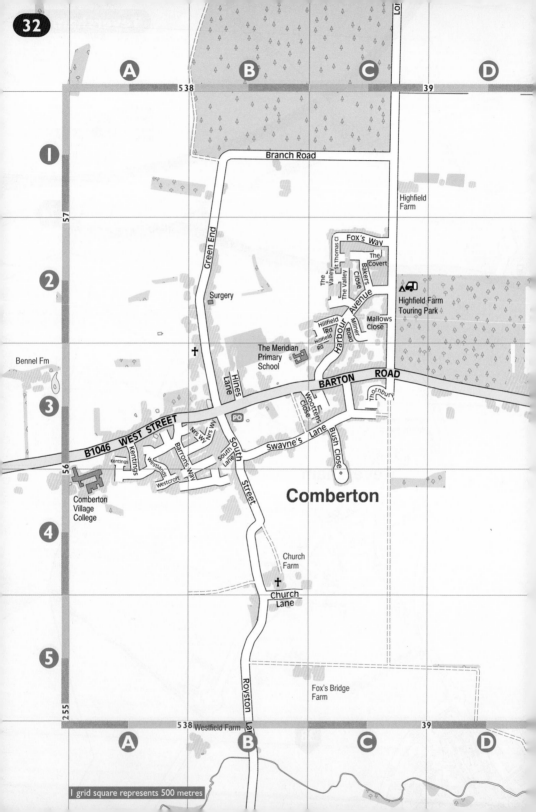

32

A   B   C   D

538   39

57

1

Branch Road

Highfield Farm

2

Green End

Surgery

Fox's Way

St Thomas Cl

The Valley

The Valley

Bakers Close

The Covert

Highfield Farm Touring Park

Mallows Close

Harbour Avenue

Milner Road

Hillfield Rd

Hillfield Rd

3

Bennel Fm

The Meridian Primary School

Hines Lane

BARTON ROAD

Thornbury

Wootten's Close

PO

WEST STREET

B1046

56

Kentings

WS Ln

WS Ln

Bartons Way

Westlands

Westcroft

South Lane

South Street

Swayne's Lane

Bush Close

Comberton

4

Comberton Village College

Church Farm

Church Lane

5

Royston Lane

Fox's Bridge Farm

255

538   Westfield Farm   39

A   B   C   D

1 grid square represents 500 metres

E 26 F G H

40 41

Comberton

I

ntchester Rd

57

Haggis Fa

2

Junction 1

3 ROAD

COMBERTON ROAD

34 Cer

Kings Grove

Hines Cl **Barton**

NEW ROAD B1046 CAMBRIDGE

PO

Barton CE
Primary School

School Lane

4

Cambridge
Road

Allens
Cl

Ivy
Fld High

Roman
Hill

Great
Close

Mailes
Cl

Street

A603

Holben
Cl

5

A603

255

A603

Bird's Farm

E F G H

40 41

MPOLE ROAD

Haslingfield Road

34 eatcases

A B 27 C BARTON D Newnham

5 42 43

Grantchester Road

A603

Queen's College Sports Ground

King's College Sports Ground

Cambri RUFC

1

57

Haggis Farm

2

Junction 12

M11

BARTON ROAD

Coton Road

Grantches

3

ROAD

Cemetery

33

CAMBRIDGE

1046

A603

Cambr e Road

4

Roman Hill

5

Coton Road

Bridle   Way

Symonds La

Broadway

Widnall Close

PO

Nutters Cl

High Street

High St

Sladwell Cl

Tabrum Cl

Stulp Fld Rd

Burnt Cl

Crome Ditch Cl

Vicarage Dr

A B C D

5 42 43

M11

Byr

I grid square represents 500 metres

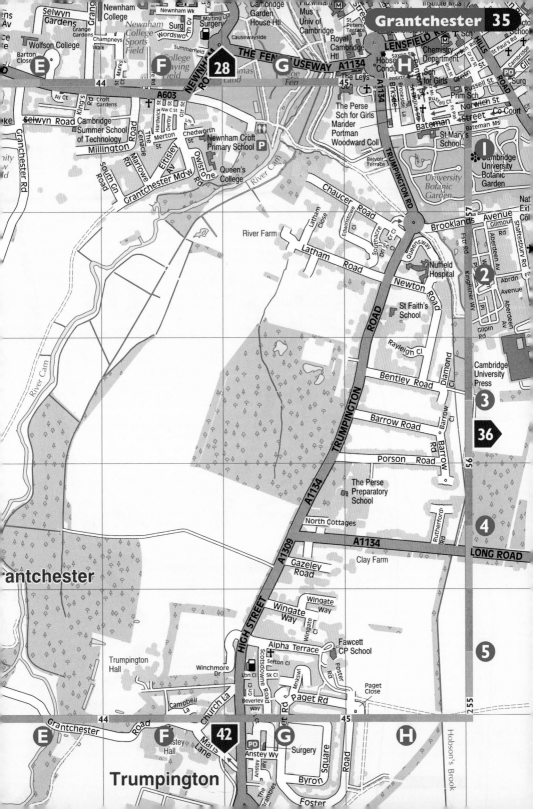

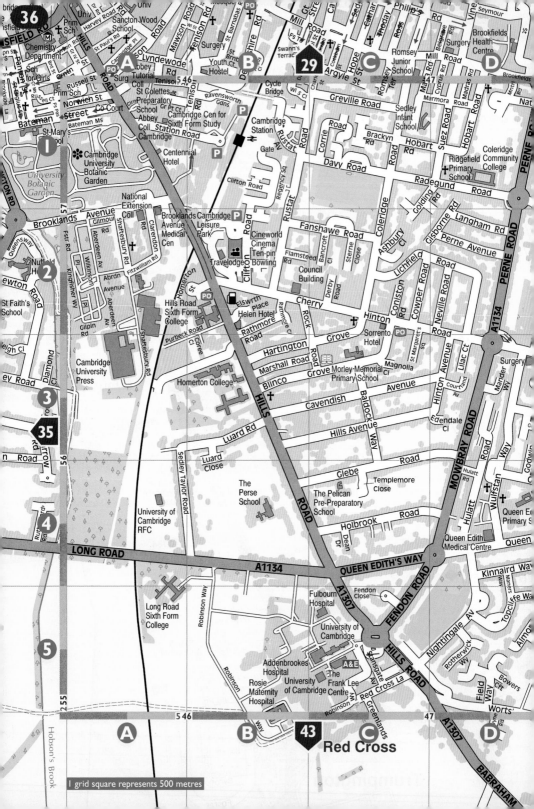

Red Cross

I grid square represents 500 metres

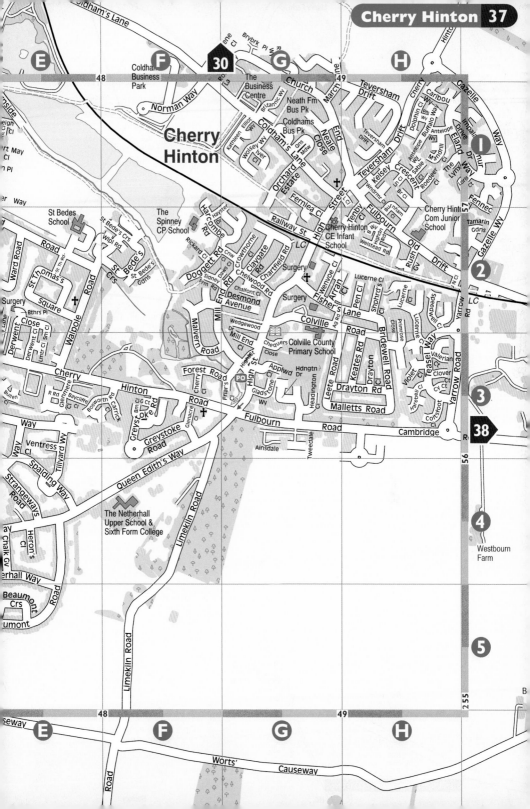

E   F   G   H

52   53

I   Wilbraham Road

40

Queens Farm

Wilbraham Road

Herring's
House

2

LC

Highfield
Gate

Apthorpe St

Station Road

Stansfield Gdns

Greater
Foxes

Northfield   Chantry

The

Church La

Harcamlow Way

3

High St

Lane

The
Haven

Health
Centre   Fulbourn
Primary
School

PO

All Saints
Road

Chaplin's

Swifts
Corner

Manor Walk

St Vigor's
Road

Hins Cl

Ludlow
Lane

School Lane

Pettit's
Close

The
Bourns

Haggis Gap

Wrights
Grove

Geoffrey Bishop
Avenue

Stonebridge

Lane

Home End

4

Harcamlow Way

Dogget Lane

Sanders
Lane

Impett's La

Balsham Road

Babraham Road

Cemetery

5

52   53

E   F   G   H

Balsham

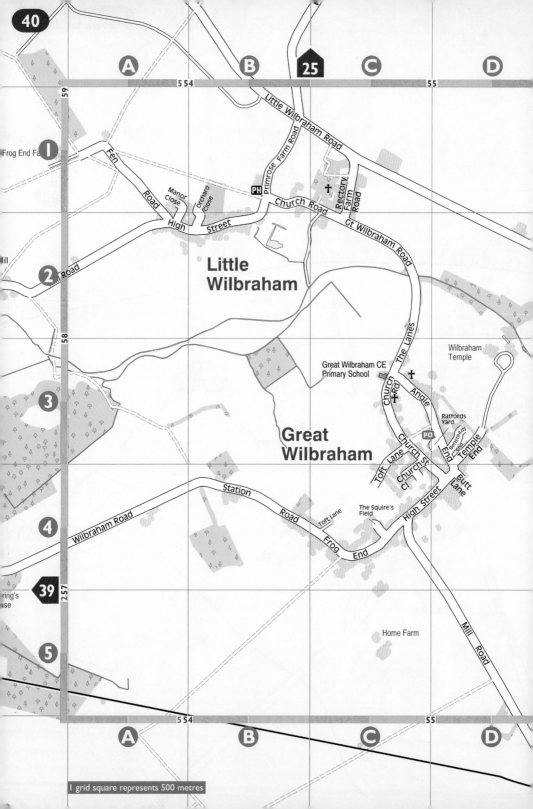

E　　　F　　　G　　　H

56　　　　　　　57

I

2

58

3

Coventry
Farm

Six
Mile
Bott

Cedar
Tree

4

A11

2 57

LC

5

56　　　　　　　57

E　　　F　　　G　　　H

University of
Cambridge

Beaumont

Almone

Nightingale

HILLS ROAD

Rotherwick Wy

Bowers

Netherhall
Farm

H

Addenbrookes
Hospital

E

Rosie
Maternity
Hospital

University
of Cambridge

The
Frank Lee
Centre

F

36

Field

G

Worts'

Alwyne Rd

47

Causeway

48

55

Limekiln

Robinson

Stansgate Av

Cross La

A&E

Greenlands

Robinson Way

Red Cross

A1307

BABRAHAM

Granham's Road

Caius
Farm

ROAD

P+🚌

Cherry

Hinton

Road

I

Pine
Wells

2

54

Hinton Wy

The Gog Magog
Golf Club

A1307

Granham's Road

Hinton Way

3

4

Hinton Way

253

Coppice Avenue

Hinton Way

Middlefield

5

Macaulay
Avenue

The Orchards

LC

Orchard Rd

Macaulay
Avenue

Wheelers

Birch Trees
Rd

Chston Rd

Orchard
Road

Hinton Way

De Freville Rd

Grn Cl

HIGH

Maris Green

E

Chaston
Rd

Millct

F

47

47

G

H

48

Haverhill Road

Tws Cl

Poplar

Shelford Park

Le

Shelford
Station

Mingle

Cemetery

TUNWELL

Frog End

Haslingfield

540 53

41

C

D

A

B

Barton Road

1

Pates Close

PO

Sidney Gdns

New

Harlton Rd

Broad Lane

Dodds Mead

The Meadows

Road

Moss Dr

Cantelupe Road

Butler Wy

Trinity Cl

River La

2

Wells

Church Street

The Knapp

Knapp Rise

Ch Wy

Cncl Bldg

Stt Yd

Fountain La

High St

Stearne's

The Hemlocks

Lilac End

Lilac Cl

Orchard Road

Badcock Rd

Chestnut Close

The Elms

52

Haslingfield Endowed Primary School

School

Lane

Back Lane

Quarry La

Chapel Hill

Haslingfield Road

3

River Cam

4

Cem

251

Chapel Hill

Charity Farm

Haslingfield Road

Butto

5

540

41

A

B

C

D

1 grid square represents 500 metres

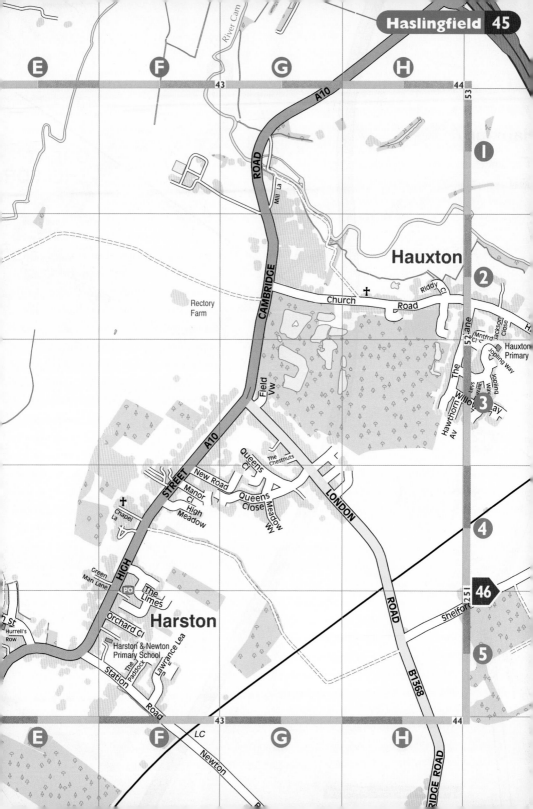

River Cam

E   F   G   H

43   44   53

A10

ROAD

I

Mill La

CAMBRIDGE

Rectory
Farm

Hauxton

2

Church   Road

Riddy

The 52 ane

Jackson
Cl

Mntfrd
Cl

Hauxton
Primary

Jopling Way

Field
Vw

Hawthorn
Av

Willow Way

Levs Walk

3

Queens
Cl

The Chestnuts

LONDON

A10

STREET

New Road

Manor
Cl

Queens
Close

Meadow Wy

High
Meadow

Chapel
La

4

ROAD

Shelford

B1251

46

HIGH

Green
Man Lane

PO

The
Limes

Harston

5

St

Hurrell's
Row

Orchard Cl

Harston & Newton
Primary School

The Paddock

Lawrance Lea

Station Road

B1368

E   F   G   H

43   LC   44

Newton

LANDRIDGE ROAD

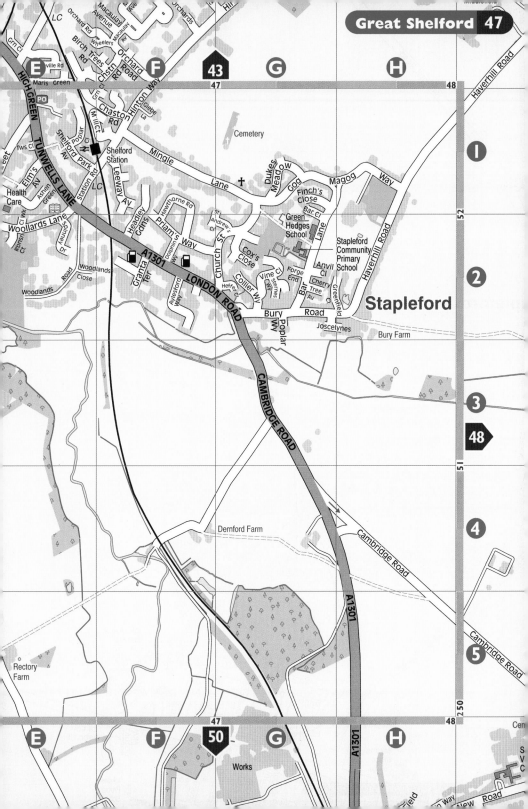

48

A   B   C   D

5 48   49

1

52

2

apleford

y Farm

River Granta

3

47

51

4

North Farm

5

Cambridge Road

West Way

Grove Rd

Middle Wy

Dales Manor Business Park

East Way

Broadmeadow La

Fairfields

Woodland Rd

Woodland Rd

Princess Drive

Edinburgh Avenue

Deal Gv

Wakelin Av

Rsd

Cl

Tm Wy

2 50

5 48   49

A   Cemetery †   B   Edinburgh Avenue   51   C   Lynton Way   Stanley Webb Cl   D

Sawston Village College

Babraham

The Limes

Roe's Cl

Churchfield Avenue

Dale Way

Holme Way

Sunderland Way

Tower Rd

Huntingdon Road

Saffron Road

Lynton Way

Icknield Primary School

Morris

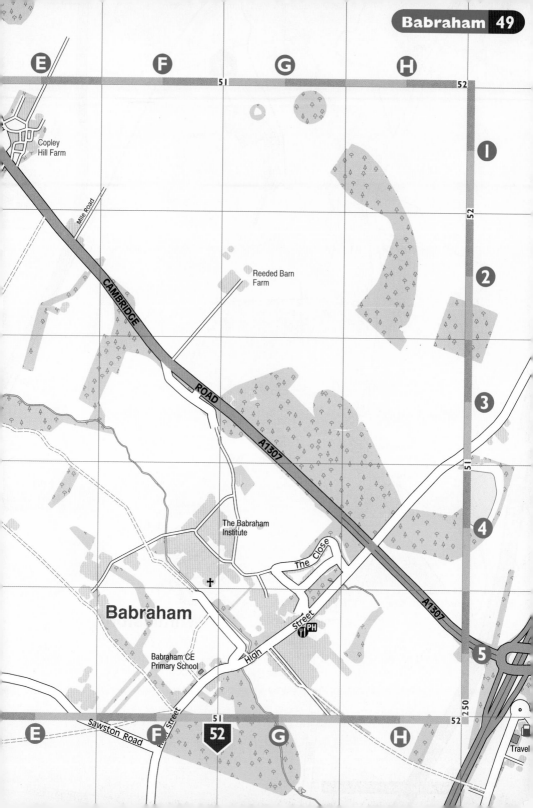

E   F   G   H

51   52

Copley
Hill Farm

Mile Road

I

52

Reeded Barn
Farm

CAMBRIDGE

2

ROAD

3

A1307

51

4

The Babraham
Institute

The Close

Babraham

High Street

PH

5

Babraham CE
Primary School

250

E   F   52   G   H

Sawston Road

High Street

51   52

Travel

50

A   B   **47**   C   D

47

5 46

50 46

1

2

3

4

5

49

48

Rectory
Farm

Works

White Field
Way

Mill Lane

A1301

The
Sta

Wells
Farm

Shelford Road

Middlemoor Road

North Road

Cemetery

Church Close

Church Lane

Gn

Lettice Martin
Croft

The Lawn

Butts

William Westley
Primary School

Old School
Lane

PO

Maynards

Scotts
Gardens

High Street

Orchard

Mill Lane

Duxford Road

Whippletree Road

Vicarage
Lane

Farm
Rise

Terrace

Ackham
Lane

Whiskins

Millfield
Farm

M11

West End

Rickards

Wren
Park

Whittlesford

A   B   **54**   C   D

5 46

47

Hill Farm Road

Royston Road

Hill

1 grid square represents 500 metres

Dales Manor Business Park

Fairfields

E Woodland Rd **F** Wicklein Av **48** **G**

bridge Road

Woodland

Princess

Edinburgh Avenue

Deal GV

Broadmeadow Rd

Grove Rd

Middle WY

East WY

Rsb

Cl

50

H

Cemetery †

Sawston Village College

Hillside

Martindale Way

Evans' Way

West Moor Avenue

The Limes

Windmill Close

Queensway

Edinburgh Avenue

Babraham Road

Churchfield Avenue

Roe's

Dale Way

Holme Way

Sundberland Road

Old Forge Way

Coldfield NWY

Link Road

John Falkner Infant School

The Baulks

PO

Selsingen Way

Cncl Bldg

Of Chalf Rd

Church Lane

†

Portobello Lane

The John Paxton Junior School

Hayfield Avenue

Vicarage Avenue

Paddock

Falkner Road

Sainfoin Close

Saffron Road

Tower Rd

Huntingdon Avenue

The Green Road

Lynton Way

Henry Morris Road

Stanley Webb Cl

Icknield Primary School

Plantation Road

SAWSTON

I

2

Chestnut Close

Town Close

Harry's Close

Street

Shingay Lane

Cambridge School of Beauty Therapy †

Prince William Way

Clover Way

Sawston Hall

St Mary's Road

St Hall Crescent

Huddleston Way

49

3

52 ▶

K Cl

High

Tannery Road

Joyce's Close

John's Acre

Skiver Close

Chamois Close

Hide Close

Hawthorn Av

Rowan Avenue

4

Meadowfield Road

London

Granta Road

Springfield Road

Brookfield Road

Brookfield Close

Park Road

Maple Avenue

North field Terrace

South Terrace

London Road

Pampisford

Brewery Road

Hammond Close

High Street Lane

Church Lane

Beech Lane

CAUSEWAY A505

Town Lane

Glebe Cr

248

London Road Industrial Estate

River Cam or Granta

E

A1301

F **55** ▼ **G**

Duxford Chapel †

Station Road West

Station Road East

ation Road West

Whittlesford Station

A505

A505

H

50

5

52

A B 49 C D

Babraham CE
Primary School

High

550 50 51

Sawston Road

High Street

1

2

49

3

51

Beech Lane

Church Lane

High Street

A505

4

CAUSEWAY A505

Town Lane

248

5

A505

Station Road

A11

A B C D
550 51

I grid square represents 500 metres

E F G H

Fourwentways Service Area

Travelodge

Cambridge Rd

I

Bourn Bridge Road

CAMBRIDGE ROAD A1307

Little Abington

urn
dge

West Field

Church

The Grip Industrial Estate

Ivan Clark's Corner

Hildersham Road

2

River Granta

Lane

Church Close

High Street

49

Great Abington Primary School

PO

Linton

3

Great Abington

Street

Meadow Walk

Road

A1307

Magna Close

High Street

Mortlock Close

Lewis Gardens

Lewis Close

4

Lewis Crs

Pampisford Road

Road

2 48

5

E F G H

Road

Chalky Road

E F 51 G H

A1301 Road
A505
49 50
47
2
A1301
3
46
4
I

Duxford Chapel
Station Road East
ation Road West
Whittlesford Station
A505

ll Lane
e

The Biggen
Hinxton Road
Fisher Cl
Road

River Cam or Granta

Hinxton

Works

LC

Duxford Road
Mill Lane
High Street
Hunts Lane
North End Road
A1301

Church Green
PH

New Road

49 50
2 45

E F G H

5

USING THE STREET INDEX

Street names are listed alphabetically. Each street name is followed by its postal town or area locality, the Postcode District, the page number, and the reference to the square in which the name is found.

Standard index entries are shown as follows:

Abbey La *WB/BUR* CB5 .... 22 B3

Street names and selected addresses not shown on the map due to scale restrictions are shown in the index with an asterisk:

Ashworth Pk *CBW* CB3 *.. 35 E1

GENERAL ABBREVIATIONS

ACC	ACCESS	CTYD	COURTYARD	HLS	HILLS	MWY	MOTORWAY	SE	SOUTH
ALY	ALLEY	CUTT.	CUTTINGS	HO	HOUSE	N	NORTH	SER	SERVICE A
AP	APPROACH	CV	COVE	HOL	HOLLOW	NE	NORTH EAST	SH	SH
AR	ARCADE	CYN	CANYON	HOSP	HOSPITAL	NW	NORTH WEST	SHOP	SHOP
ASS	ASSOCIATION	DEPT	DEPARTMENT	HRB	HARBOUR	O/P	OVERPASS	SKWY	SKY
AV	AVENUE	DL	DALE	HTH	HEATH	OFF	OFFICE	SMT	SUN
BCH	BEACH	DM	DAM	HTS	HEIGHTS	ORCH	ORCHARD	SOC	SOC
BLDS	BUILDINGS	DR	DRIVE	HVN	HAVEN	OV	OVAL	SP	SP
BND	BEND	DRO	DROVE	HWY	HIGHWAY	PAL	PALACE	SPR	SP
BNK	BANK	DRY	DRIVEWAY	IMP	IMPERIAL	PAS	PASSAGE	SQ	SQL
BR	BRIDGE	DWGS	DWELLINGS	IN	INLET	PAV	PAVILION	ST	ST
BRK	BROOK	E	EAST	IND EST	INDUSTRIAL ESTATE	PDE	PARADE	STN	STA
BTM	BOTTOM	EMB	EMBANKMENT	INF	INFIRMARY	PH	PUBLIC HOUSE	STR	STR
BUS	BUSINESS	EMBY	EMBASSY	INFO	INFORMATION	PK	PARK	STRD	STR
BVD	BOULEVARD	ESP	ESPLANADE	INT	INTERCHANGE	PKWY	PARKWAY	SW	SOUTH V
BY	BYPASS	EST	ESTATE	IS	ISLAND	PL	PLACE	TDG	TRA
CATH	CATHEDRAL	EX	EXCHANGE	JCT	JUNCTION	PLN	PLAIN	TER	TERR
CEM	CEMETERY	EXPY	EXPRESSWAY	JTY	JETTY	PLNS	PLAINS	THWY	THROUGH
CEN	CENTRE	EXT	EXTENSION	KG	KING	PLZ	PLAZA	TNL	TUN
CFT	CROFT	F/O	FLYOVER	KNL	KNOLL	POL	POLICE STATION	TOLL	TOLL
CH	CHURCH	FC	FOOTBALL CLUB	L	LAKE	PR	PRINCE	TPK	TURN
CHA	CHASE	FK	FORK	LA	LANE	PREC	PRECINCT	TR	TR
CHYD	CHURCHYARD	FLD	FIELD	LDG	LODGE	PREP	PREPARATORY	TRL	T
CIR	CIRCLE	FLDS	FIELDS	LGT	LIGHT	PRIM	PRIMARY	TWR	TC
CIRC	CIRCUS	FLS	FALLS	LK	LOCK	PROM	PROMENADE	U/P	UNDER
CL	CLOSE	FM	FARM	LKS	LAKES	PRS	PRINCESS	UNI	UNIVER
CLFS	CLIFFS	FT	FORT	LNDG	LANDING	PRT	PORT	UPR	UF
CMP	CAMP	FTS	FLATS	LTL	LITTLE	PT	POINT	V	
CNR	CORNER	FWY	FREEWAY	LWR	LOWER	PTH	PATH	VA	VA
CO.	COUNTY	FY	FERRY	MAG	MAGISTRATE	PZ	PIAZZA	VIAD	VIAL
COLL	COLLEGE	GA	GATE	MAN	MANSIONS	QD	QUADRANT	VIL	L
COM	COMMON	GAL	GALLERY	MD.	MEAD	QU	QUEEN	VIS	V
COMM	COMMISSION	GDN	GARDEN	MDW	MEADOWS	QY	QUAY	VLG	VILL
CON	CONVENT	GDNS	GARDENS	MEM	MEMORIAL	R	RIVER	VLS	VI
COT	COTTAGE	GLD	GLADE	MI	MILL	RBT	ROUNDABOUT	VW	V
COTS	COTTAGES	GLN	GLEN	MKT	MARKET	RD	ROAD	W	
CP	CAPE	GN	GREEN	MKTS	MARKETS	RDG	RIDGE	WD	W
CPS	COPSE	GND	GROUND	ML	MALL	REP	REPUBLIC	WHF	WH
CR	CREEK	GRA	GRANGE	MNR	MANOR	RES	RESERVOIR	WK	
CREM	CREMATORIUM	GRG	GARAGE	MS	MEWS	RFC	RUGBY FOOTBALL CLUB	WKS	W
CRS	CRESCENT	GT	GREAT	MSN	MISSION	RI	RISE	WLS	W
CSWY	CAUSEWAY	GTWY	GATEWAY	MT	MOUNT	RP	RAMP	WY	
CT	COURT	GV	GROVE	MTN	MOUNTAIN	RW	ROW	YD	
CTRL	CENTRAL	HGR	HIGHER	MTS	MOUNTAINS	S	SOUTH	YHA	YOUTH HO
CTS	COURTS	HL	HILL	MUS	MUSEUM	SCH	SCHOOL		

POSTCODE TOWNS AND AREA ABBREVIATIONS

CBE/LIN .... Cambridge east/ Linton	CBN .... Cambridge north	CBW .... Cambridge west	SAFWN .... Saffron Walden north	WB/BUR............ Waterbea Bur
	CBS .... Cambridge south	NMKT .... Newmarket		

nry Morris Rd
CBN CB4 13 F4
CBS CB2 51 G1
rbert St CBN CB4 29 E1
rcules Cl CBN CB4 19 H2
reward Cl CBN CB4 13 F4
ron's Cl CBE/LIN CB1 37 E4
e Herons CBN CB4 7 E3
rring's Cl
WB/BUR CB5 24 B3
rschel Rd CBW CB3 28 B4
rtford St CBN CB4 28 D2
ks La CBW CB3 18 B2
le Cl CBS CB2 51 F3
ghdene Rd
CBE/LIN CB1 37 H2
gh Ditch Rd
WB/BUR CB5 31 G1
ghfield Av CBN CB4 19 H5
hfield Cl CBS CB2 54 D4
hfield Ga
BE/LIN CB1 39 E2
hfield Rd CBN CB4 19 F1
h Gn CBS CB2 47 E1
h Meadow CBS CB2 45 F4
hsett CBS CB2 3 J7
h St CBE/LIN CB1 31 G4
BE/LIN CB1 37 G2
BE/LIN CB1 39 E3
BE/LIN CB1 53 G4
BN CB4 4 C3
BN CB4 7 E4
BN CB4 11 H1
BN CB4 13 E3
BN CB4 15 E5
BN CB4 20 C5
BN CB4 29 G1
BS CB2 35 G5
BS CB2 47 E1
BS CB2 50 C4
BS CB2 51 F3
BS CB2 52 B1
BW CB3 18 B1
BW CB3 26 D3
BW CB3 33 G4
BW CB3 34 D4
BW CB3 44 B2
AFWN CB10 55 G5
B/BUR CB5 9 G4
B/BUR CB5 21 F5
B/BUR CB5 21 H1
B/BUR CB5 22 B3
B/BUR CB5 25 H3
hworth Av CBN CB4 20 A5
a St CBN CB4 28 D1
ersham Rd
BE/LIN CB1 53 H2
crest CBW CB3 10 B4
Farm Rd CBS CB2 50 B5
field Rd CBW CB3 32 C3
s Av CBE/LIN CB1 36 C3
side CBS CB2 51 E1
s Rd CBS CB2 3 H6
es Cl CBW CB3 33 F4
es La CBW CB3 32 B3
ton Av CBE/LIN CB1 36 D3
ton Rd CBE/LIN CB1 38 C3
ton Wy CBS CB2 47 F1
xton Rd CBS CB2 55 E4
ton Rd CBN CB4 19 F4
BN CB4 28 C1
adly Rd CBW CB3 19 E5
bart Rd CBE/LIN CB1 36 D1
bsons Acre CBS CB2 42 D5
bson St CBE/LIN CB1 3 F3
ben Cl CBW CB3 33 G5
brook Rd
BE/LIN CB1 36 C4
land St CBN CB4 28 D2
mans Cl
BE/LIN CB1 39 E4
ymount
BE/LIN CB1 * 3 K3
ytrees CBW CB3 10 B4
me Cl CBN CB4 11 H2
mefield Cl CBN CB4 13 F4
me Wy CBS CB2 51 F1
wood Cl CBN CB4 19 F4
ne Cl CBN CB4 13 E3
ne End CBE/LIN CB1 39 F4
ne Farm Cl CBN CB4 5 H1
nefield Cl CBN CB4 13 F4
nerton St CBS CB2 36 B2
Homing
B/BUR CB5 30 C2
ey Hl CBW CB3 2 C1
ey Hill Ms CBW CB3 2 C1
per St CBE/LIN CB1 29 G4
e St CBE/LIN CB1 29 H5
kins Cl CBN CB4 20 B4
ningsea Rd
B/BUR CB5 21 G4
ward Cl
B/BUR CB5 30 B1
ward Rd
B/BUR CB5 30 B1
ves Pl CBW CB3 18 D5
gate Rd CBN CB4 19 F3
lett Wy
B/BUR CB5 25 G2

Huddleston Wy
CBS CB2 51 G2
Hulatt Rd CBE/LIN CB1 36 D4
Humberstone Rd
CBN CB4 29 F2
Humphreys Rd
CBN CB4 19 H4
Humphries Wy
CBN CB4 15 E4
Huntingdon Rd
CBS CB2 51 G1
CBW CB3 10 A2
CBW CB3 11 F5
CBW CB3 18 B4
CBW CB3 28 B1
Huntley Cl
WB/BUR CB5 30 C1
Hunts La SAFWN CB10 55 H5
Huntsmill CBE/LIN CB1 38 D4
Hunts Rd CBS CB2 54 D4
Hurrell Rd CBN CB4 19 F4
Hurrell's Rw CBS CB2 45 E5
Hurrys Cl CBS CB2 51 E2
Hurst Park Av CBN CB4 19 H5

I

Iceni Wy CBN CB4 19 G3
Ickleton Rd CBS CB2 54 D4
Impala Dr CBE/LIN CB1 38 A1
Impett's La
CBE/LIN CB1 39 F4
Impington La CBN CB4 13 F4
Inveran CBE/LIN CB1 3 K3
Inverness Cl CBN CB4 20 B5
Ivan Clark's Cnr
CBE/LIN CB1 53 G2
Ivatt St CBN CB4 7 F2
Iver Cl CBE/LIN CB1 37 G1
Ivy Fld CBW CB3 33 G4
Izaak Walton Wy
CBN CB4 20 D5

J

Jackson Cl CBS CB2 46 A2
Jackson Rd CBN CB4 20 A3
Jack Warren Gn
WB/BUR CB5 30 C2
James Nurse Cl
CBE/LIN CB1 37 H2
James St WB/BUR CB5 3 J2
Jedburgh Cl CBN CB4 19 H3
Jenyns Cl WB/BUR CB5 25 G1
Jermyn Cl CBN CB4 19 G4
Jesus La WB/BUR CB5 3 F2
Jesus Ter CBE/LIN CB1 3 H3
JJ Thompson Av
CBW CB3 27 H3
John Clarke Ct
CBN CB4 20 B4
John's Acre CBS CB2 51 F3
John St CBE/LIN CB1 3 H4
Jolley Wy CBN CB4 20 A4
Jopling Wy CBS CB2 46 A2
Jordans New Yd
CBS CB2 2 E2
Joscelynes CBS CB2 47 G2
Josiah Ct WB/BUR CB5 9 H4
Joyce's Cl CBS CB2 51 F3
Jubilee Cl WB/BUR CB5 9 F4

K

Kathleen Elliot Wy
CBE/LIN CB1 37 G1
Kay Hitch Wy CBN CB4 13 E5
Keates Rd CBE/LIN CB1 37 H3
Kelsey Crs CBE/LIN CB1 37 H1
Kelvin Cl CBE/LIN CB1 37 E3
Kendal Wy CBN CB4 20 C4
Ken's Wy CBN CB4 15 E5
Kentings CBW CB3 32 A3
Kent Wy CBN CB4 20 A3
Kerridge Cl
CBE/LIN CB1 29 G4
Kestrel Cl CBN CB4 7 F2
Kettles Cl CBN CB4 11 H2
Keynes Rd
WB/BUR CB5 30 B1
Kilmaine Cl CBN CB4 20 A2
Kingfisher Cl CBS CB2 51 F3
Kingfisher Wy CBN CB4 7 E2
CBS CB2 35 H2
Kings Gv CBW CB3 33 G4
Kings Hedges Dr
CBN CB4 * 20 A2
King's Hedges Rd
CBN CB4 19 G3
Kings Mill La CBS CB2 46 D2
King's Pde CBS CB2 2 E4
King's Rd CBW CB3 35 E1
Kingston St
CBE/LIN CB1 29 G5

King St CBE/LIN CB1 3 F3
CBN CB4 5 H1
Kinnaird Wy
CBE/LIN CB1 36 D4
Kinross Ms CBN CB4 * 20 B5
Kinross Rd CBN CB4 20 B5
Kintbury CBS CB2 54 D4
Kirby Cl CBN CB4 20 A5
Kirby Rd WB/BUR CB5 9 H3
Kirkwood Rd CBN CB4 20 A3
Knapp Ri CBW CB3 44 A3
The Knapp CBW CB3 44 A2
Knights Wy CBN CB4 15 E4

L

Laburnum Cl CBN CB4 29 F1
Lacey's Wy CBS CB2 54 D3
Lacks Cl CBN CB4 7 E4
Lady Jermy Wy
CBE/LIN CB1 31 F4
Lady Margaret Rd
CBW CB3 2 C1
Ladywalk CBN CB4 4 C2
Lambourn Cl CBS CB2 35 G5
Lamb's La CBN CB4 7 E4
Lammas Fld CBW CB3 35 F1
Landbeach Rd
CBN CB4 15 E4
Lander Cl CBN CB4 14 D4
The Lanes CBE/LIN CB1 40 C3
The Lane CBS CB2 45 H3
Langdale Cl
CBE/LIN CB1 37 H1
Langham Rd
CBE/LIN CB1 36 D2
Lansdowne Rd
CBW CB3 27 H2
Lantree Crs CBS CB2 42 B2
Lapwings Cl
CBE/LIN CB1 31 F4
Larkin Cl CBN CB4 20 B4
Larmor Dr CBW CB3 2 A1
Latham Cl CBS CB2 35 G2
Latham Rd CBS CB2 35 G2
Latimer Cl WB/BUR CB5 30 C2
Laundress La CBW CB3 2 D5
Laundry La
CBE/LIN CB1 37 E3
Lavender Rd CBN CB4 20 B3
The Lawns CBW CB3 28 A3
The Lawn CBS CB2 50 C4
Lawrance Lea CBS CB2 45 F5
Lawrence Cl CBW CB3 18 B2
Lawrence Wy
CBN CB4 20 A3
Lawson Cl CBN CB4 13 E3
Laxton Wy CBN CB4 20 D4
Lee Cl CBN CB4 7 E4
Lees Wy CBW CB3 18 B1
Leete Rd CBE/LIN CB1 37 G3
Leeway Av CBS CB2 47 F1
Lemur Dr CBE/LIN CB1 38 A1
Lensfield Rd CBS CB2 3 F7
Lents Wy CBN CB4 20 D5
Leonard Cl
WB/BUR CB5 30 C1
Leopold Wk CBN CB4 7 F4
Lettice Martin Cft
CBS CB2 50 D4
Lewis Cl CBE/LIN CB1 53 G4
Lewis Crs CBE/LIN CB1 53 G4
Lexington Cl CBN CB4 19 F5
Leyburn Cl
CBE/LIN CB1 37 H1
Leys Av CBN CB4 19 H4
Leys Rd CBN CB4 20 A5
Leys Wk CBS CB2 46 A2
Lichfield Rd
CBE/LIN CB1 36 C2
Lilac Cl CBW CB3 44 B2
Lilac Ct CBE/LIN CB1 36 D3
Lilac End CBW CB3 44 B2
Limekiln Rd
CBE/LIN CB1 37 F5
The Limes CBS CB2 45 F5
CBS CB2 51 F1
Limetree Cl
CBE/LIN CB1 37 E3
Linden Cl CBN CB4 28 C1
Lingholme Cl CBN CB4 19 F5
Lingrey Ct CBS CB2 42 B1
Link Rd CBS CB2 51 F1
The Linnets CBN CB4 7 E3
Linton Rd CBE/LIN CB1 53 G3
Lion Yd CBS CB2 * 2 E4
Little Meadow
CBW CB3 10 A5
Little St Mary's La
CBS CB2 2 E6
Little Wilbraham Rd
CBE/LIN CB1 40 B1
WB/BUR CB5 25 F4
Livermore Cl CBN CB4 20 A3
Lode Av WB/BUR CB5 9 G5
Lode Rd WB/BUR CB5 25 G2
Logan's Wy CBN CB4 29 G2
London Rd CBS CB2 45 G4

CBS CB2 47 F2
CBS CB2 51 F4
Lone Tree Av CBN CB4 19 F2
Long Meadow Rd
WB/BUR CB5 23 E3
Long Reach Rd
CBN CB4 20 D5
Long Rd CBS CB2 36 A4
Longstanton Rd
CBN CB4 11 G1
Longview Ter
CBN CB4 * 28 C1
Longworth Av
CBN CB4 29 G2
Loris Ct CBE/LIN CB1 37 H1
Lovell Rd CBN CB4 20 B3
Love's Cl CBN CB4 13 F5
Lowbury Crs CBN CB4 11 G1
Lower Park St
WB/BUR CB5 2 E2
Low Fen Drove Wy
WB/BUR CB5 31 F1
Luard Cl CBS CB2 36 B4
Luard Rd CBS CB2 36 B3
Lucerne Cl CBE/LIN CB1 37 H2
Lucketts Cl CBN CB4 13 E3
Ludlow La CBE/LIN CB1 39 E4
Lyles Rd CBN CB4 7 E4
Lyndewode Rd
CBE/LIN CB1 3 J7
Lyndhurst Cl CBN CB4 14 D5
Lynfield La CBN CB4 29 G1
Lynton Wy CBS CB2 51 G1
The Lynx CBE/LIN CB1 37 H1

M

Macaulay Av CBS CB2 43 F5
Macfarlane Cl CBN CB4 13 F5
Mackenzie Rd
CBE/LIN CB1 3 K5
Madingley Rd CBW CB3 27 G2
Madras Rd CBE/LIN CB1 36 D1
Magdalene Cl CBN CB4 4 D3
Magdalene St CBW CB3 2 D1
Magna Cl CBE/LIN CB1 53 G3
Magnolia Cl
CBE/LIN CB1 36 C3
Magrath Av CBN CB4 28 D2
Maids Cswy CBE/LIN CB1 3 H3
Mailes Cl CBW CB3 33 G4
Main St WB/BUR CB5 24 C2
Maio Rd CBN CB4 20 A5
Maitland Av CBN CB4 20 C4
Malcolm Pl CBE/LIN CB1 3 F3
Malcolm St CBE/LIN CB1 3 F2
Malden Cl WB/BUR CB5 30 B2
Males Cl CBN CB4 7 F2
The Mallards
WB/BUR CB5 * 29 G2
Malletts Rd
CBE/LIN CB1 37 G3
Mallows Cl CBW CB3 32 C2
Malta Rd CBE/LIN CB1 36 C1
Malting La CBW CB3 2 C6
Maltsters Wy CBN CB4 29 G1
Malvern Rd
CBE/LIN CB1 37 F2
Mander Wy
CBE/LIN CB1 36 D3
Mandrill Cl CBE/LIN CB1 37 H1
Maners Wy
CBE/LIN CB1 36 D4
Mangers La CBS CB2 54 D3
Manhattan Dr CBN CB4 3 J1
Manor Cl CBE/LIN CB1 40 A1
CBS CB2 45 F4
Manor Ct CBW CB3 2 A6
Manor Farm Cl
CBN CB4 11 H1
Manor Farm Ct CBN CB4 7 E4
Manor Farm Rd
CBW CB3 12 B5
Manor Pk CBN CB4 12 D3
Manor Pl CBE/LIN CB1 3 F3
Manor Rd CBS CB2 46 C2
Manor St CBE/LIN CB1 3 F3
Manor Wk CBE/LIN CB1 39 F3
Manse Dr CBN CB4 6 D4
Mansel Wy CBN CB4 19 H4
Mansfield Cl CBN CB4 14 D5
Maple Av CBS CB2 51 F4
Maple Cl WB/BUR CB5 25 H3
The Maples
CBE/LIN CB1 38 D3
March La CBE/LIN CB1 37 G1
March's Cl CBE/LIN CB1 38 D3
Marfleet Cl CBS CB2 42 D4
Margett St CBN CB4 7 F3
Mariner's Wy CBN CB4 29 G2
Marion Cl CBW CB3 28 B1
Maris Gn CBS CB2 43 E5
Maris La CBS CB2 42 A1
Markby Cl CBS CB2 54 D4
Market Hl CBS CB2 2 E4
Market Pas CBS CB2 2 E3
Market Ri
CBE/LIN CB1 * 36 B2

Market St CBS CB2 2 E4
Markham Cl CBN CB4 20 A2
Mark's Wy CBW CB3 18 C1
Marlborough Ct
CBW CB3 2 A6
Marlowe Rd CBW CB3 35 F1
Marmora Rd
CBE/LIN CB1 36 C1
Marshall Rd CBS CB2 36 B3
Marshall's Cl
CBE/LIN CB1 31 F4
Martindale Wy CBS CB2 51 E1
Martingale Cl CBN CB4 19 F4
Maryland Av
WB/BUR CB5 23 G3
Matthew Parker Cl
CBN CB4 8 C5
Mawson Rd CBE/LIN CB1 3 J7
Mayfield Rd CBW CB3 18 C2
Maynards CBS CB2 50 C4
Mays Wy CBN CB4 20 D5
Meadow Farm Cl
CBN CB4 12 A1
Meadowfield Rd CBS
CB2 51 E3
Meadowlands Rd
WB/BUR CB5 30 C2
The Meadows CBW CB3 44 B2
Meadow Wk
CBE/LIN CB1 53 G3
Meadow Wy CBS CB2 45 G4
Mead Vw CBN CB4 11 G2
Melvin Wy CBN CB4 12 D3
Mercers Rw
WB/BUR CB5 29 H1
Mere Wy CBN CB4 19 H4
Merlin Pl CBN CB4 * 20 D2
Merryvale CBS CB2 42 B2
Merton Pk
WB/BUR CB5 * 9 G4
Merton Rd CBN CB4 13 E4
Merton St CBW CB3 35 F1
Metcalfe Rd CBN CB4 19 G5
Michaelmas Pl
CBN CB4 * 28 D1
Michael's Cl CBW CB3 18 B1
Middlemoor Rd
CBS CB2 50 A4
Middle Wy CBS CB2 48 C5
Midwinter Pl CBN CB4 * 29 F1
Mile Rd CBS CB2 49 E2
Milford St CBE/LIN CB1 29 G4
Millards La
WB/BUR CB5 22 C3
Mill Ct CBS CB2 47 E1
Mill End Cl CBE/LIN CB1 37 G3
Mill End Rd
CBE/LIN CB1 37 G2
Millers Yd CBS CB2 * 2 E5
Millington La
CBW CB3 * 35 F1
Millington Rd CBW CB3 35 E1
Mill La CBN CB4 13 G2
CBS CB2 2 D5
CBS CB2 45 G1
CBS CB2 50 D4
CBS CB2 55 E3
SAFWN CB10 55 G5
WB/BUR CB5 23 G2
Mill Rd CBE/LIN CB1 3 J5
CBE/LIN CB1 40 D5
CBN CB4 12 A1
CBN CB4 19 E1
CBS CB2 44 D5
WB/BUR CB5 9 F5
WB/BUR CB5 22 B3
Mills La CBN CB4 4 D4
Mill St CBE/LIN CB1 3 J6
Mill Wy CBW CB3 34 D5
Milner Cl CBS CB2 51 E2
Milner Rd CBW CB3 32 C2
Milton Rd CBN CB4 20 C3
Minerva Wy CBN CB4 19 H2
Mingle La CBS CB2 47 F1
Minter Cl
WB/BUR CB5 24 C3
Missleton Ct
CBE/LIN CB1 36 D3
Misty Mdw
WB/BUR CB5 30 B1
Molewood Cl CBN CB4 19 F4
Moncrieff Cl CBN CB4 19 H3
Monkswell CBS CB2 35 G5
Montague Rd CBN CB4 29 F2
Montgomery Rd
CBN CB4 19 H4
Montreal Rd
CBE/LIN CB1 36 D1
Montrose Cl CBN CB4 19 H3
Moore Cl CBN CB4 20 B4
Moorfield Rd CBS CB2 54 D2
More's Meadow
CBS CB2 42 D5
Morgans CBN CB4 7 E4
Morleys Pl CBS CB2 * 51 F2
Mortimer Rd
CBE/LIN CB1 3 J5
Mortlock Av CBN CB4 20 C4
Mortlock Gdns
CBE/LIN CB1 53 G4